P9-DOE-446

The Sleepwalker's Son

Also by Bill Meissner:

Learning to Breathe Underwater

The Sleepwalker's Son

Bill Meissner

OHIO UNIVERSITY PRESS
ATHENS, OHIO
LONDON

© Copyright 1987 by William Meissner.
Printed in the United States of America.
All rights reserved.

LIBRARY OF CONGRESS CATALOGING IN PUBLICATION DATA

Meissner, William, 1948—
    The sleepwalker's son.

    Poems.
    1. Title.
PS3563.E38S5   1986   811'.54   86-16252
ISBN 0-8214-0854-2
ISBN 0-8214-0855-0 (pbK.)

*for Christine, the one who could wake me
and for Nathan*

TABLE OF CONTENTS

THE SECRET OF AMERICA

LIVING IN HOUSES TOO NEAR THE RIVER

ACKNOWLEDGMENTS

I'd like to thank my mother and father for their support of my writing. Thanks also to Jack Driscoll, poet and friend.

I would like to thank the McKnight Foundation for a $6,000 Loft-McKnight Poetry Award, and the Minnesota State Arts Board for a $5,500 Individual Artist Award which supported the writing of this book.

Several of the poems in this manuscript received awards in national contests:
"Husband Shoveling Snow from the Roof," Second Prize in the 1982 Billee Murray Denny Poetry Awards.
"Waking to a Fall Down the Stairs," Honorable Mention in the 1982 Billee Murray Denny Poetry Awards.
"Waking to a Fall Down the Stairs," Honorable Mention in the 1982 *Milkweed Chronicle* Awards.

The poems in this collection have previously appeared in the following publications:
POETRY: "So Many Americans, Driving Late on Country Roads"; POETRY NORTHWEST: "Climbing into My Father's Skin," "The Psychometrist and His Woman"; CAROLINA QUARTERLY: "The Voice Gymnast," "Drunk Man Walking the Trestle above the River"; THREE RIVERS POETRY JOURNAL: "After Going off the Road during a Blizzard," "Twisters"; KANSAS QUARTERLY: "The Baseball Lover"; SOUTHERN POETRY REVIEW: "The Ice Walkers"; NORTHEAST: "End of the World: Hearing that Snow Collapsed the Alpine Cafe Roof," "The Education of Martin Halsted"; MIDWEST QUARTERLY: "Hometown Widow Whose Laundry Never Gets Clean" (as "Hometown Widow"); INDIANA REVIEW: "The Magician, Sawing His Woman in Half"; "The Spring Father Stopped Snowing"; POETRY NOW: "Champions"; LOUISVILLE REVIEW: "The Stormy Night Burt Worthy An-

nounced the Tornado Warning"; QUARTERLY WEST: "Husband Shoveling Snow from the Roof"; CHARITON REVIEW: "Son of a Traveling Salesman," "The Ann Landers Poem I"ve been Meaning to Write All These Years: Finally Written After Hearing Ann and I Were Both Born in Sioux City, Iowa"; MILKWEED CHRONICLE: "Waking to a Fall Down the Stairs"; SUNDOG: "The Secrets of America"; MID AMERICAN REVIEW: "1963, The First Kill: After Dad Shot the Pheasant That Flew into Barbed Wire," "The Sons and Daughters Talk of the Drowned Fathers"; CHELSEA: "Poem for the Insects in Fall"; MINNESOTA MONTHLY: "The Shoe: When Our 19-Month-Old Son Lost His Tennis Shoe in Lake Superior," and "After Our 30th Birthdays, My Wife and I Walk to the Center of the Lake," "The Great Minnesota Ski Mask Story."

Rescuing the Dreamer

CLIMBING INTO MY FATHER'S SKIN

It's like crawling into a cave
I always knew was there
but never explored.
I remember putting my head
into his salesman's briefcase
when I was young.
This time the bright eye
I entered pulls
away, a helium balloon.

Farther down, the musty air wheezes,
sighs trapped for years
in frayed motel rooms.

Some boy has been here before.
Burned matches in a corner,
a tennis shoe, unreadable scratchings
on the walls. This is far

enough. Turning to find my way
out, I walk along a narrow black stream
where pale hands are rising,
sinking.

I find myself tiptoeing
into the water: like the time I slipped
my tiny feet into his large dark shoes, it is
deeper than I expected. Up
to my knees, my waist,
I see the opening again—
a circle of sky cut with a dull car key,
a blue mouth singing a melody
I know by heart
but have never heard before.

As I go
under, my arms,
thick as my father's,
reach above the surface,
then return
to embrace me.

HUSBAND SHOVELING SNOW FROM THE ROOF

Already the tarpaper of the sky
is leaning on him.
For the first time he notices
the closeness of the stars:
pinheads of ice
prickling the skin of his forearm.

In the living room his wife could not know
this one shovelful is
heavier than anything he's
lifted in his life.
He tries to heft it over the
edge, anticipating

the distant explosion.
But all he hears
is this avalanche beginning
inside his body, this weight
of snow no man could

stop. Falling headfirst,
he understands the stupidity of ladders.
It was enough
to have tried to keep this roof
from collapsing, enough
to hold up her sighs,
like a dozen winters, with his
bare hands.

Even the drift
twenty feet beneath him is
amazed, the way he plunges soundlessly
into its white heart.

Later she gazes out an upstairs window:
the same chimneys nudging
white arteries into the night.
He's below, eyes open toward her.
She stares until she can see no
more, her face a circle of steam
the wind can never wipe away.

REMEMBERING THAT CITY BUS RIDE IN QUITO, ECUADOR

I saw it first: a large black dog
ambling into the cobblestone street.
Inside the battered bus
in my metal seat, I kept quiet.
I didn't speak their language.
I squeezed the handrail
that was worn to a shine.

The dog moved slowly, a shadow
hiding from the sun's path.
The bus accelerated, shifted;
passengers' heads snapped back.

As if it were blind,
the dog didn't even glance at
the bumper inches away.

For an instant,
a silence
filled with dull claws.

Then the thud, a yelp, the hollow
thumping as the dog rolled
under the bus.

I watched the
sound, a metallic heartbeat,
traveling the length of
concave floorboards, coming
closer and closer to me
until I wished I were deaf,
until it vibrated beneath
the soles of my shoes.

Years later, there are still nights
I see that dream approaching.
    When it reaches me, I let go,
    my bony elbows and knees rolling and rolling
    as it wraps around me
    choking and comforting
    like a blanket of exhaust.

THE VOICE GYMNAST

> "Stan the Loudmouth" has mastered 300 sound
> effects and 100 voices. His siren imitation
> reaches 128 decibels. . . .

In bed, his voice makes sounds
no one could imagine: a herd
of frightened horses, an owl in flight
in a sleetstorm, thunder
that nearly breaks the glass
of his sleep.

He sees himself in a schoolyard at six:
kids turned their heads
when his lips stumbled
on an imitation of dripping water.
Now his mouth fills with
world records.
County fairs by the dozen hire him
just to hear his grain elevator,
his thresher.

He practices five hours a day.
His throat becomes a tornado
tearing the silence of his life
to shreds.

He could live the rest of his years
without uttering a single human word,
still see the people that surround him
nodding, smiling, understanding everything.

Tonight his bedroom walls echo,
a thousand impressions
he could never master while awake,
a thousand grackles clinging to invisible wires.

In a quiet field of dream,
he leans back and shouts his name.
Six miles away, windows shatter.

DRAWING SWASTIKAS ON THE FOGGED WINDOWS
OF ST. JOSEPH'S GRADE SCHOOL, 1959

After school we cleaned bruised boards,
clapped white explosions from erasers.
The nun sat in her solitude;
in ours, we drew bombers in notebooks.

Sisters, we meant nothing by it.
We were only apprentices at war—
gray blood something that grinned at us from the screen.
Buds on the girls and triggers excited us.
We dreamed Nazis: how they could scrape off
the horizon with their fingernails.

We didn't understand the world
was once a mountain, ready to avalanche.
For us history was that pine forest
behind the playground, filling with snow.

Noon hours in the basement,
we rationed cigarettes, laughed
at bomb shelter signs, fingered dirty pictures
smuggled in bag lunches
until the boilers hissed.

After an hour she dismissed us.
We saw fish in the aquarium by the cloakroom
swimming in squadrons.
At home we drew on our arms with red Magic Marker.

Sisters, no enemy planes ever tore the air
above your school. It was just a target
for the wrecking ball, a decade later.
When the first bricks collapsed,
ghosts of the kids we once were
    cowered in the basement,
        the lights blacked out,
            the windows steamed.

THE SONS AND DAUGHTERS TALK OF THE DROWNED FATHERS

Your bodies were never recovered.
We remember coffinless funerals, gravel
popping under tires like hollow acorns.
For years your white shirts surfaced
in the middle of our dreams.

All we wanted was to be assured you weren't still
on the bottom, your chests pinned down by fishing rods.
All we wanted was to press our palms to your bloated faces,
close your closed eyes.

For days the hooks searched with rusted smiles.
As though you were some exotic game fish,
they trolled and trolled the lakes for you,
not giving up until your foreheads froze over.

Now our lives are nothing more than
leaves fallen on water.

We need you, fathers:
all we wanted was to be near you once more,
to have the chance to drift at your sides a long time
and say nothing.

POEM FOR THE INSECTS IN FALL

1

I have seen them:
crickets hiding beneath porches,
the black glass of their songs
broken into splinters.
Moths shivering
among pale grass blades
while this season approaches,
the blades of a lawn mower.

2

Some nights I crouch in the cold deep grass
of my sleep, hiding from
dawn. Somewhere a cricket
dreams the sound of a clock ticking,
and I dream the dream of moths:
a dance around the warm lightbulb
of the moon.

3

By midmorning, insects lift stiff wings
above pavement, dot
the windshields,
surprised pinheads of death.

4

Warm afternoons I would save them all,
gather them into my shirt pocket,
or I would drive
back and forth on the highway,
accelerating into them
until I can no longer see,
their tiny opaque brushstrokes coating the windshield
like first frost.

THE SLEEPWALKERS

1

Dad, as a boy you sleepwalked
to you father's radio headphones,
put them on and listened,
listened.
Did you hear your dead grandfather talking,
or your future son,
music too beautiful for waking?
Or was it just the late night static,
an ice storm caught between your temples?

You never woke—
your father watched you lift the headset off,
tiptoe back upstairs, curl
in bed around your secret.

2

I am the son who walks
into rooms of himself, recognizes
no furniture. I am the son
who climbs your nightmare's winding stairs.

3

Sometimes, inhaling the half sleeping air,
I walk past your bedroom and
wonder, Dad, what you were listening for.
Wonder if you hear this whole family,
this houseful of gentle, terrified sleepers
near you, our whimpers useless as mattress coils
trying to poke holes in your dream.

Wonder if you'll wake
with that same silence
piling up like crystal in your ears.

Reasons We Can't Fall Asleep

THE EDUCATION OF MARTIN HALSTED

We taught you, Martin. In sixth grade the three of us taught
your marshmallow hands to harden,
taught your cheeks the color of bruises.

In the alley behind a wooden shed,
one by one we punched your face
until the eggs of your eyes broke.

You never wanted to fight anyone.
It's just that your face was a window
we always wanted to fling a rock through.

In junior high you moved to another town.
Your mother sent you to an institution—
weird in the head, everyone said.

Last time I saw you was sophomore year at the theatre.
Back for the weekend, you told me
how much you loved to draw circles with a pen
on the back of your left hand.
You held it toward me:
too close in the near dark, you smudged my cheek.

Sometimes, when I go back to town,
I drive up and down that alley.
Sometimes I want to get out
of the car, rub my palm on the shed,
feel the slivers searching.

The three of us are grown now, work in different cities.
Though we don't know it, Martin, you're the reason
we can't fall asleep some nights.
And in the mornings, our hands on the wheel,
you're the scars on our knuckles
we never grew out of.

NOVEMBER, 1963, THE FIRST KILL:
AFTER DAD SHOT THE PHEASANT THAT FLEW INTO
BARBED WIRE

He eased the bird into the inside pocket
of his hunting jacket. He told me he could feel
the warmth fading. Excited,
I looked inside: a blood stain
spreading.

Before dinner we cleaned the bird in the basement.
Down stuck to Dad's wrists
like small grey puffs of smoke.

A year later, Dad would sell the shotgun,
buy a .22, just for target practice.
I blasted tin cans to feathers.

Dad didn't talk much at the table.
He was chewing the pain,
swallowing slowly, his stomach accepting the meat.

All through the meal
he picked small black pellets
from his mouth, placed each
on the side of his plate with a
click.

THE STORMY NIGHT BURT WORTHY ANNOUNCED THE TORNADO WARNING

It wasn't funny, Burt.
That tornado you were searching for
could have killed us all.

We were crazy to hear it
over our radios. Your voice
crackled and scraped behind a cloud of static
as you read the warning from an FCC card.

Some of us flattened like water
under beds; some of us,
wrists wrapped in rosaries,
froze, prayed for sunlight at 10 p.m.
When the lights blinked out,
the whole town
heard your voice on the radio die,
orange tubes glowing a moment.

We could have killed ourselves,
rushing down fruit cellar stairs
with weak flashlights, stubby candles.
Your wife bumped a jar of beets:
the bloody star expanded on dank cement.

You leaned into your mike through it all, Burt—
wetting your voice with an empty glass,
your white hair standing up, as it always did,
lifted by some invisible wind.

Later everyone figured you invented the sighting.
But that night, the station off the air, you
dozed, jerked awake, mumbled into the mike,
saving our lives
long after the storm had passed.

The top of his head evaporates into morning mist.
He's a blot of ink against the horizon,
a stain waiting to be erased.

If he fell, no one in this city would know,
the white scar quickly healing above him,
his name washed from his own lips.

He pauses, wavering. He might be imagining
a son, a daughter who hear
the sound of distant train whistles in their sleep.

Fog weighs his shoulders
like so much heavy wool until
he can carry it no more,
until he falls

to his knees and stares between the ties.
The ducks, heading south for winter,
could smooth a thousand headaches
the way they fly so gracefully: their wingtips
throbbing inches above the water
without ever touching it.

SPEEDY

(Assistant Manager, Al Ringling Theatre)

Speedy, every Friday and Saturday night,
when your small body rushed down
the raucous aisle, the entire theatre
tilted toward you.

Our junior high feet were big
on the theatre seats in front of us.
We loved it
that you had two thumbs
on your right hand.
Even when you pointed those six fingers at us,
we smarted off, we pointed back,
proud of our normal hands.

We cheered our thrown steelies,
like bullets of gunslingers,
each time they punched holes
through the innocent screen.
We laughed as the famous lovers necked.
We reached deeper into our popcorns,
butter slick on the balls of our thumbs.

Once I crumpled up a Milk Duds box,
pelted you in the back of your square head.
When you spun around, I stared right at you;
you never suspected it was me.
Your flashlight was useless
as the dark side of the moon.

We never really hated you, Speedy.
You were just our shooting gallery penguin,
our tin silhouette sliding back and
forth in front of black and white heroes.

CHAMPIONS

Some of us never made it.
We never needed to go that far.
Some of us broke our legs trying, some
broke our lives.
Drive into your man, the coach shouted,
turn his bones to powder.
We practiced until we were taut pillars of wire
holding the dusk above this corn-bordered field.
We thanked the twilight that stopped salt
from swarming to our lips.

Think of your opponent as the enemy, he said,
his voice a steel trigger.
Our knees were rippling flags.
A million boys in China
would beg to sweat for fun.
So, alone in our lines, we learned to love it.

If you're a champion, he told us, show him
how real bruises feel.
We'd spend days thinking about it,
not caring what we wasted.

We did it for our coach.
We did it for ourselves, we did it
for the whole town.
When he finally nodded us toward showers,
crickets cheered as if they knew we'd forget
all these scores in a few years.

Those Friday nights, when we took the field,
we were too ready; beneath floodlights,
our muscles glowed
like filaments. And we killed
those guys. We
killed them.

HOMETOWN WIDOW WHOSE
LAUNDRY NEVER GETS CLEAN

She's had enough of this town,
so she paints all the windows
of her house black.

She was tired of her neighbors' voices
scratching against the glass,
tongues filed hard
as the points of butcher knives.
Tired of always watching
for first snow, the way it smothers
her fingerprints on the begonias.

The quilted robe she wraps around herself is solitude.
This is the cloister no one can visit
except the preacher on Sunday radio,
church music flying the hallway,
a canary with one wing.

She will go outside only to hang another load
of her dead husband's shirts on the line.
Through a fingernail crescent in the
kitchen window, she sees one hanger
blow off. The others on the line
bob nervously, black
wire frowns waiting
as the wind un-
hooks them
one by
one.

END OF THE WORLD: HEARING THAT SNOW
COLLAPSED THE ALPINE CAFE ROOF

So Otto's broad white apron
finally drifted over him.
You remember him standing behind the counter
holding two Frostie root beers,
the foam overflowing, sliding
down his wrist for
ten years.

And the summer night a million moths
landed on the roof of the Alpine,
trying to lift the whole building
from this town. Our town

is being destroyed
from the outside, everyone says.
Otto remembered the day
the brick streets were stunned
with hot tar, the time
the courthouse statue's granite chest
bled blue ink.

    The newspaper editor rushes
    into the barber shop gasping
    about the new interstate
    and the barber nicks
    the back of your head,
    your perfect crewcut.
    You stare at yourself in the wood-rimmed
    double mirrors: white cape beneath your chin,
    you become smaller in frame after frame
    until you look like the moths
    clinging near the red neon sign
in the front window of the Alpine.

How could Otto have known
this place would give
in to the sadness of plastic booths,
formica tables, piped-in silence?
He always stood polishing stainless steel dispensers,
sliding his toweled fist into thick caves
of malted milk glasses.
You and your brother sat
on soda fountain stools
lost in the tiers of candies,
Swisher Sweets, air fresheners shaped like keys.
To preserve all this from the weight
of the world, the way those symmetrical
rows of green olives inside the gallon jars
will last for a century.

After the big snowfall, the plaster smiles
just before the rafters fall
to their knees, Otto
covered in an avalanche
of foam.

And the olives roll onto the sidewalk
like hundreds of unblinking eyes
which arrive the next morning
to stare at the latest accident.

The Secret of America

THE ANN LANDERS POEM I'VE BEEN MEANING TO WRITE ALL THESE YEARS: FINALLY WRITTEN AFTER HEARING ANN AND I WERE BOTH BORN IN SIOUX CITY, IOWA

Ann, no wonder your advice was always so clear:
it was something like the sound of bells in fog
as cows grazed along the Sioux City bluffs.

You told me as a teen to beware the automobile—
it's a bedroom on wheels and we rarely get good mileage.
What our country needs is more coffee,
you kept saying, and a better sense of smell.

Your newsprint replies, like black nets, have caught
a thousand marriages as they fell.

Now your columns I've saved crumble
like dried butterfly collections.
This is the new age, Ann: Nebraska has nuclear pockmarks,
housewives flatten foreheads against computer screens.

Still, you keep answering letters,
dishing out those hamburger casseroles of advice.

When you got your divorce, a hole opened
in the middle of Iowa, large
as the inky scream you dreamt.

Thousands of residents gave up their subscriptions,
threw themselves in and were never seen again,
except in the obituary columns next to yours.

Even the cows, huddled together in trucks
aimed for the Sioux City stockyards,
pushed wet noses through wooden slats
and called your name. Ann,

I wanted to stop reading you, too,
but your smudged face keeps reappearing at breakfast
each time I wrap the coffee grounds,
your words sliding across my American thumbs
harmlessly as paper cuts.

TWISTERS

What else is there to do but
aim his pickup into this fallow field
and spin?
The concentric ruts
are the circles under his eyes.
Dust devils curl behind the truck—
he imagines them swirling
like cyclones down Main Street,
tearing the tin grain elevator apart,
bringing the water tower to its knees.

He curses the grey screen that formed
between him and his woman last night—
the way she would only talk
through a locked hollow-core door,
his lips feeling the wood vibrate.

He cranks the wheel until
his elbows ache, accelerates
until his toes are blisters.

He believes dust will turn to gold,
believes he could spin and
spin, digging deeper into the land, spin
until he carves a shallow lake
in the center of this parched field, spin
the rest of his life,
but the engine
dies.

Climbing onto the hood,
he watches the last of the dust:
a small twister
the soft breeze tears apart
before it reaches the edge of town.

LATE WINTER: THE ICE WALKERS

All afternoon they slide tennis shoes
toward the place where the river ice

thins to nothing
        as their hair will,
        thirty years later,
        when they glance in the mirror and,
        for an instant, remember
this walk.

Their tattered toes inch
forward, wishing eggshell ice
into pavement.
This is the thrill of being too near the
edge, of crossing
that fragile white bridge
of yourself.

Each spring there will be a thousand excited boys
on the still-frozen rivers,
a thousand mothers waiting for
the door slam
that always rattles the china. Thirty years
        later the ice walkers sit down for dinner,
        not noticing the steam from their soup
        might be the same steam that danced from the river.
        Daily they cross thick gray paths to their jobs,
        never think of falling through.

        Tonight it's hockey on the TV.
        The glazed glow of the set
        almost churns up some memory of the danger
        they tiptoed on. They sink

        deeper into the couch,
        think of asking their wives for another whiskey,
        hearing the cubes in their drinks settling.

THE BASEBALL LOVER

So far it's a no hitter.
She's still on the couch, staring at quiz shows,
he's in the corner, oiling his glove
with his tongue.

This is the tension of extra innings—
all day he's waited on deck,
counting the circles chalked
on his brain.

She complains he wears his yellow baseball cap
too much. Sometimes he even sleeps with it
on his face like an egg yolk,
while her breathing makes the sound of wind
through empty bleachers.
All night dreams flow from the cap's brim:
    He's sliding toward home plate
    and the slide never stops—through the dugout,
    under the grandstand, across the sandlot,
    into the skin of his childhood,
    the seat of his pants burning
    like birth.

At the commercial he switches on the Braves' game.
Someone is trying to steal home—
his legs
are the wings
of anxious birds.
He will never
move in slow
motion, not
even in the
replay. Here
comes the pitch
here comes

the runner,
he slides
> next to her on the couch,
> begins whispering sweet baseball scores
> into her ear.

THE PSYCHOMETRIST AND HIS WOMAN

Though he is a perfect stranger,
he knows you this well:
just by holding the locket he found on your driveway,
he can read all the words tattooed
on the underside of your throat.

His knuckles steam.
If only he could feel your stocking,
he'd tell you how far
you've walked today,
if smoke ever circles your thighs.

You are not one to let any man caress your secrets.
Yet he has turned you inside out many times
in his dream; he'd like to leave fingerprints
on your every emotion,
to explore each fold and crease.

At breakfast, he's just an ordinary man, dropping
banana peels into the garbage.
Only when he starts his car does something
click, only then does he believe
he has traveled a million miles
beneath your face.
In that instant you are there,
next to him on the front seat.
He reaches to find your hand.
The sound of your whole life resonates
through the guitar strings in his wrist.

THE GREAT MINNESOTA SKI MASK STORY

1

It's always those Minnesotans, shoveling snow
winter after winter alongside identical masked neighbors.
Sometimes they begin to wonder who they really are,
where their sidewalk actually ends.

2

Indoors, Minnesotans make a habit of taking off ski masks
within eyeshot of a mirror,
making certain their faces
have not turned into 85% orlon, 15% nylon.

3

Other residents eat their dinner with ski masks on.
Whole families sit around the table
with maroon or navy faces,
slurping spaghetti through frayed mouth holes.
At such moments these families are very close.

4

Prominent citizens, donning ski masks for the first time,
have been known to stand in front of picture windows
naked.

5

Some Minnesotans even sleep wearing ski masks,
rolling over and over
in the snowdrifts of their dreams, waking up
still warm.

6

By spring, ski masks are peeled off for the season—
on closet shelves, they hold the face shapes
of their owners.

And some owners' faces retain ski mask seams
well into summer. Strangers on the street ask
Just take off your ski mask?

It is at such times Minnesotans yearn
for their old masks,
yearn for just a trace of snow in July,
anxious to slip on their second faces,
anxious to be
nobody again.

AN AMERICAN DECADE
The Sixties. The Automobile Crash Tests.

The skull is always the first to make impact.
In the slow motion film on television, fragments
of glass splash beautifully
from the windshield.

The bald head emerges
smoothly, a baby's crown.

Other times we see their whole bodies,
dressed in fatigues, collapsing gradually
against dash or front seat,
drivers' chests sinking deeper and
deeper into steering columns.

In our living rooms, sometimes we must
look away, unable to bear
the thought of the wounded.

But they keep the same expressionless faces
as if being unable to stop
is simply their destiny,
as if they know
the bayonets of glass will slash only
polyethylene, as if
they're certain
they will not be the ones
who will die.

SON OF A TRAVELING SALESMAN

I knew nothing of him.

But before I was born, I could feel his hands,
turning me round and round
inside the womb.

After I got my license I noticed
a desire to drive smooth highways,
an unexplainable affection for
vegetable slicers, vacuum cleaners, encyclopedias.

In high school I developed optimism, optimism
shining like pots and pans that would not tarnish.
I never let my pride's fingernails
be blued by slamming doors.

Once, drunk, I looked for him—
drove up and down streets,
block after block blurring,
pages torn from a phone book.

Father, why did you leave your shoe
in my door so many years?

Daydreaming at my desk, I see myself
at sixteen, the way my hands fit so easily
around the skeleton of a steering wheel.

How much I seemed to have ahead of me then—
each day was another door to be knocked on,
each morning another stranger's smile:
as inviting and
distant as luck.

THE MAGICIAN, SAWING HIS WOMAN IN HALF

She can see the flash of the magician's blade
even through the closed curtain.
It's her cue: he traces
the edge of the saw with his thumb.

On the table in a bikini, she
is covered with a wooden box.
Her skin senses night.

He begins the stroking, thinking
a woman loves the cool steel
kiss close to her groin.
She's thinking *to sever a woman is easy*
as slicing a melon. When he finally cuts

through, she separates with a gasp,
light spilling from her torso.

For a few seconds he has two women:
one that will never run away,
the other that cannot stop his hand
from gliding up a thigh.

Afterwards in the dressing room
she massages her stomach
to erase his fingerprints,

remembering that terrifying sensation
when the two halves of herself
were wheeled to opposite sides of the stage,
remembering the strong wave of his hand
that made her almost whole again.

SO MANY AMERICANS, DRIVING LATE ON
COUNTRY ROADS

> The most likely time for a fatal automobile
> accident is one a.m. Sunday morning. Often these
> accidents involve a single car with one
> passenger.   —newspaper article

It's always this place that calls you. You
turn a corner at the edge of town,
the wheel in your hands the outline of a shape
you no longer understand.

Like the dozens of drivers all over America
who parallel you tonight on other country roads,
you stare through a horizon of curved glass:
the asphalt deepens into a starless sky.
Your wallet is full; you believe you could accelerate
for years. You don't realize you're following a blinking line
of drivers, their names in smeared ink
of Monday morning obituaries.
Their histories yellow in basements,
like your headlights fading beyond the gravel shoulder.

The speedometer turns over. The dashboard
flares. This place always calls
you, its voice softer
than your velour seats, calls you
to close your eyes
and meet it head on.

It's the simple end that is best.
Beyond that first sharp curve,
a single tree waits.

Never a witness. Perhaps
a lone dog whose ears straighten at the

impact. It limps the other direction,
deeper into woods, while twigs
tick like an overheated engine cooling.

THE SECRETS OF AMERICA

They die and are born and go on dying,
their feet never leaving their yards.

Mornings, they spread their margarine smoothly,
don't remember the darkness that pooled
in the backs of their skulls while they slept.
They put extra cream in their coffee.

Fathers and mothers won't mention their sons drive
on country roads at night without headlights,
daughters lift pleated skirts
above their heads like overcast skies.

Everyone believes the ghosts of their ancestors enter
through their shoes as they garden.
They picture themselves walking barefoot near the church.
Downtown, young wives gaze through their reflections
at naked mannequins.

Before dinner, they brown their roasts
on both sides. Recipes are funneled into electrical wires,
squeezed along by the feet of blackbirds.

In time, they'll tell you, their houses will
sink into the ground until the whole town's
a flat plain again,
a place for pioneers to discover.

They'll tell you this is America
idling in their garages, America steaming on their plates.

America in their back yards,
like trousers hanging on the clothesline in the wind,
the hollow legs climbing and dancing and
falling still all afternoon.

*Living in Houses Too
Near the River*

THE SPRING FATHER STOPPED SNOWING

That spring, Father stopped snowing.
He let out a long sigh, the last gust of wind
after a blizzard. He dropped his newspaper,
turned his palms upward, his face flushed pink again.

None of us believed he had stopped—
the TV screen still vibrated with white flecks,
countertops were covered by flakes of pie dough,
the dining room table was drifted over with lace.

But it was true— all that snow began to melt,
the basement filling with a foot of water.
After the lights went out, he waded toward the fuse box,
a candle in front of his forehead.
Not dangerous at all, he told us, water up to his waist.

We believed him, until the flood lifted the house
from its foundation.

He looked thinner
as he took us to the swaying attic, opened closets,
showed us family photo albums:
great grandmothers and grandfathers we'd never seen,
their eyes frosted over.

Trying to lighten the house, he dropped them
out the window
as water climbed the steep stairs.

On the roof, he handed us each our baby picture,
gave Mom their wedding photo.
Keep these in your pockets, he told us,
they might buoy you up.

He slid down the shingles onto a cake of ice,
pushed away from the house with a gaunt smile.

Crying, we waved to him, the distance growing
between us as he floated down river on that white pupil
that must have seen him more clearly than we ever did.

AFTER GOING OFF THE ROAD DURING THE BLIZZARD

He still stares into the windshield.
He'd drive and keep driving
at seventy, his vision
burning holes through decades
of snowstorms.

His wife still clutches the dash
as if this skid across the slick surface
of winter will
never end.

After a few hours, the dome light's
glow shrinks, a
flashlight dropped
into a deep pool
of cloth. The radio
wraps itself in static,
a sound like footsteps
brushing across sand.

Now they can begin
the love dance
they have forgotten.
The back seat imagines the panting
that steams windows to silk.

In the dark they reach
to find each other
with that same joy a search party
feels, after days,
when it discovers the missing travelers
beneath a drift,
their pulsebeats
still jarring the snow
from their wrists.

It's almost like going to heaven
head over heels. To survive this one,
you must tuck your head
under, break your fingers
of their bad habit of
always wanting to hang on.

Slowing yourself will only
sharpen your elbows, resisting
might expose the lightbulbs
of your kneecaps.

Forget that your bones are icicles;
think of them as the bones of an infant—
streams where snails could glide on their reflections.
Let go
your name, your birth date,
those things that keep tripping you
like shoes two sizes too large.

Perhaps your spine will become
a smooth stairway.
Perhaps you'll get by with only a few bruises
on your tongue, shadows
left over from words
you always wanted to say.

Halfway down, you almost enjoy this
descent, your body absorbing
all its unnecessary angles.
You learn everything there is to know
about falling, believe you could tumble
down stairway after stairway
in your sleep, never dent
a single dream.

AFTER OUR 30th BIRTHDAYS, MY WIFE
AND I WALK TO THE CENTER OF THE LAKE

This winter is always too long.

We brush away powdery snow: ice,
a foot thick but still clear.

We think we can see to the bottom
where minnows circle, fireflies in a jar,
where small pages of light are turning.

We love the simplicity of this ice;
if only we could always see this way—

we crouch down on hands and knees
like children peering at the world
through their first magnifying glass.

LIVING IN HOUSES TOO NEAR THE RIVER:
FOUR EXPLANATIONS OF HOME

1

As we drive out of town,
my two-year-old asks—What is home?
Already he feels it.

I want to tell him it's like the spiral
a snail carries on its back.
Once the shell's emptied, the ocean pretends
to live inside it.

2

Home: I want to tell him it's a place
I've searched for, my palms sliding
across a splintered wall.

    I can picture each house where I've lived:
    maps deepening in the plaster.
    I remember childhood: Kool Aid
    evaporating from sidewalks.

Home: sometimes I think it illuminates my forehead
   while I sleep like light from a collapsed star.

3

The house we live in settles each year,
inch by inch, toward the river.
One day it will float seaward, an ancient ship,
knots in the boards like blind sailors' eyes.

4

Son, I can't explain it to you.
Every time I try, it becomes a riddle,
my tongue a spiral.

The best I can do is repeat one small story
which must be true:
        once, looking for home, I drove back
        to the town where I grew up.
        The house was gone, but
        I could still feel something,
        the way an amputee still feels warm tingling
        in the leg he lost years ago.

THE SHOE: WHEN OUR 19-MONTH-OLD SON
LOST HIS TENNIS SHOE IN LAKE SUPERIOR

The first time you wore it
you just had to kick

it off, your foot growing,
growing as if in a zoom lens.

On my stomach, I stretched across
lava rocks, my aching fingertips watching as

it filled with toes of water,
took its first step

into a dark green dropoff.
You watched from above,

wiggling your bare foot in the sharp wind
as if you'd kick off shoe after shoe,

risk your father's life, giggling.
Back in the cabin your mother and I

talk of the shoe strolling for years
a few inches from the bottom.

talk of the salmon fisherman, miles from shore,
who reels it in, laugh

at ourselves for glancing out the window
to see if the shoe has drifted back.

Beneath the bare bulb,
we notice the grey on each other's temples.

You're long asleep in the crib,
dreaming of a shoe

floating, like a fish tired of water, to the
surface. A boy's fingers pick it up.

Though it's much too small for him,
he slides it on and it fits.

FATHER AND SON SONG FOR ONE, TWO OR THREE VOICES

1

Son to His Father, Who Says He's Too Old to Dance

Father, your legs don't have to turn spectacular shapes in air.
Dancing is easy as kicking your shoes
into the closet at the edge of each afternoon.

Father, the world's not so fragile
it will fall out from under you.
The dance can be sturdy as your workbench,
the music can be the sound of pounding
nails, or a saw's edge shimmering
just before it meets the wood.

All your feet need to do is carve
a simple word in the carpet,
a word you can stand on the rest of your years.

2

Father to His Son, After the Birth of the Grandson

Let me tell you this, son: the first steps you took
were like new words to me. I heard them
whispered on the car radio, and my soles ached
as I drove. As I drove,
the distance between our feet
told us how much we loved each other.

Forgive me the days I was gone—
a salesman, the highway wrapped around my forehead
like the grey silk ribbon on my hat.

Son, let me tell you: each time I
returned, I noticed your eyes darkening with a color
I couldn't identify, like water flowing beneath ice.

The time I came home and found you dancing alone,
I wept for all the miles I'd traveled
without my feet touching the earth.

3

The Grandson's Waltz

I'll always remember that night
when I was still too young to walk:
Dad perched my tiny curled feet
on top of his own, then danced me,
laughing, around the living room.
The static sparking
beneath my father's socks
        brought back a memory before birth—
        as if I recalled the womb flickering
        each time another hinge of
        leg or ankle
        connected.
I wanted to dance that way for hours.
I want to dance that way now,
and even when my father's dancing slows
to a shuffle, slows
to a twitch of bare feet while he naps,
the fading music still fluttering
inside each toe.

Bill Meissner directs the creative writing program at St. Cloud State University in Minnesota. His poetry has won numerous awards, including an NEA Fellowship, a Loft-McKnight Award, and a Minnesota State Arts Board Fellowship. His poetry and fiction have been published widely, and his first book of poems is *Learning To Breathe Underwater*. He lives in St. Cloud with his wife, Christine, and their son, Nathan.